Rising to the Call of Leadership

Kay Arthur, David & BJ Lawson

PRECEPT MINISTRIES INTERNATIONAL

WATERBROOK
PRESS

Rising to the Call of Leadership
Published by WaterBrook Press
12265 Oracle Boulevard, Suite 200
Colorado Springs, Colorado 80921

ISBN 978-0-307-45769-1

Published in the United States by WaterBrook Multnomah, an imprint of the Crown Publishing Group, a division of Random House Inc., New York.

WATERBROOK and its deer colophon are registered trademarks of Random House Inc.

Printed in the United States of America
2014

10 9 8 7

SPECIAL SALES
Most WaterBrook Multnomah books are available at special quantity discounts when purchased in bulk by corporations, organizations, and special-interest groups. Custom imprinting or excerpting can also be done to fit special needs. For information, please e-mail SpecialMarkets@WaterBrookMultnomah.com or call 1-800-603-7051.

HOW TO USE THIS STUDY

This small-group study is for people who are interested in learning for themselves more about what the Bible says on various subjects, but who have only limited time to meet together. It's ideal, for example, for a lunch group at work, an early morning men's group, a young mothers' group meeting in a home, a Sunday-school class, or even family devotions. (It's also ideal for small groups that typically have longer meeting times—such as evening groups or Saturday morning groups—but want to devote only a portion of their time together to actual study, while reserving the rest for prayer, fellowship, or other activities.)

This book is designed so that all the group's participants will complete each lesson's study activities *at the same time*. Discussing your insights drawn from what God says about the subject reveals exciting, life-impacting truths.

Although it's a group study, you'll need a facilitator to lead the study and keep the discussion moving. (This person's function is *not* that of a lecturer or teacher. However, when this book is used in a Sunday-school class or similar setting, the teacher should feel free to lead more directly and to bring in other insights in addition to those provided in each week's lesson.)

If *you* are your group's facilitator, the leader, here are some helpful points for making your job easier:

- Go through the lesson and mark the text before you lead the group. This will give you increased familiarity with the material and will enable you to facilitate the group with greater ease. It may be easier for you to lead the group through the instructions for marking if you, as a leader, choose a specific color for each symbol you mark.

- As you lead the group, start at the beginning of the text and simply read it aloud in the order it appears in the lesson, including the "insight boxes," which appear throughout. Work through the lesson together, observing and discussing what you learn. As you read the Scripture verses, have the group say aloud the word they are marking in the text.

- The discussion questions are there simply to help you cover the material. As the class moves into the discussion, many times you will find that they will cover the questions on their own. Remember, the discussion questions are there to guide the group through the topic, not to squelch discussion.

- Remember how important it is for people to verbalize their answers and discoveries. This greatly strengthens their personal understanding of each week's lesson. Try to ensure that everyone has plenty of opportunity to contribute to each week's discussions.

- Keep the discussion moving. This may mean spending more time on some parts of the study than on others. If necessary, you should feel free to spread out a lesson over more than one session. However, remember that you don't want to slow the pace too much. It's much better to leave everyone "wanting more" than to have people dropping out because of declining interest.

- If the validity or accuracy of some of the answers seems questionable, you can gently and cheerfully remind the group to stay focused on the truth of the Scriptures. Your object is to learn what the Bible says, not to engage in human philosophy. Simply stick with the Scriptures and give God the opportunity to speak. His Word *is* truth (John 17:17)!

RISING TO THE CALL OF LEADERSHIP

What makes a leader a leader? What is it that makes some people leaders while others are just the person in charge?

Dr. Martin Luther King Jr. once wrote: "There was a time when the church was very powerful—in the time when the early Christians rejoiced at being deemed worthy to suffer for what they believed. In those days the church was not merely a thermometer that recorded the ideas and principles of popular opinion; it was a thermostat that transformed the mores of society."[1]

In leadership what makes the difference between a thermometer and a thermostat? A thermostat sets the

---

[1] Martin Luther King Jr., "Letter from Birmingham Jail," 16 April 1963. Copyright © The Estate of Martin Luther King, Jr.

agenda; a thermometer simply represents what is already in place. Dr. King was describing the church, but the description fits the individual leaders within the body also.

Leadership is tough. But God calls us to be leaders—in our homes, in our communities, in our churches, and ultimately in our world.

So what does God expect of those He places in positions of authority? What characteristics set apart the truly effective leader in contrast to the person who just happens to be out front? And how can you be the leader God has called you to be?

These are some of the questions we want to examine by the light of God's Word as we look at the lives of four Old Testament leaders. Their examples offer powerful insights about the hallmarks of great leadership as well as the pitfalls that can undermine our influence and effectiveness.

Our prayer is that this study will give you a basic understanding of the characteristics we need as men and women of God who are called to live with biblical authority and strength in a world that desperately needs trustworthy leaders.

One of the greatest difficulties a leader faces is choosing the right course of action when others challenge the rules or undermine his authority. This week we're going to look at two men who faced this situation and responded in very different ways.

OBSERVE

In the last days of the times of the judges of Israel, Eli served as the high priest at Shiloh. His sons, Hophni and Phinehas, served as priests under his leadership.

Leader: *Read aloud 1 Samuel 2:12–17.*
  • *Have the group say aloud and mark every reference to* **the sons of Eli** *or* **the priest's servant,** *including pronouns and synonyms, with a* **P.**

As you read the text, it's helpful to have the group say the key words aloud as they mark them. This way everyone will be sure to mark every occurrence of the word, including any synonymous words or phrases. Do this throughout the study.

1 SAMUEL 2:12–17

12 Now the sons of **P** Eli were worthless [worthless] men; they did not **P** know the LORD [didn't know the Lord]

13 and the custom of the priests with the people. When any man [didn't know custom] was offering a sacrifice, the priest's **P** servant would come while the meat was boiling, with a three-pronged fork in **P** his hand.

14 Then he would **P** thrust it into the pan, or kettle, or caldron, or pot; all that the fork brought up the priest would take for himself.

Thus they did in Shiloh to all the Israelites who came there.

15 Also, before they burned the fat, the priest's servant would come and say to the man who was sacrificing, "Give the priest meat for roasting, as he will not take boiled meat from you, only raw."

16 If the man said to him, "They must surely burn the fat first, and then take as much as you desire," then he would say, "No, but you shall give it to me now; and if not, I will take it by force."

17 Thus the sin of the young men was very great before the LORD, for the men despised the offering of the LORD.

DISCUSS

• What did you observe about Eli's sons from the vivid description in verses 12 and 13?

• Briefly discuss the behavior of Eli's sons as described in verses 13–16. What does this reveal about their character?

INSIGHT

The book of Leviticus describes in detail the Law of Moses and the sacrificial system. Leviticus 7 tells us the fat of the sacrifices belongs to the Lord and is to be burned. Leviticus 10:14–15 explicitly describes the priest's portion of the sacrifice. The practices described in 1 Samuel 2 are clearly in violation of God's instructions.

• According to verse 16, even the ordinary worshiper knew that God's portion took precedence over the priest's share; yet how did Eli's sons respond when confronted about their violation of the Law?

OBSERVE

Leader: Read aloud 1 Samuel 2:22–25. Have the group...

- mark each reference to **Eli,** including pronouns, with an **E.**
- mark each reference to **Eli's sons,** including pronouns, with a **P.**

DISCUSS

- What did you learn about Eli from this passage?

- What had Eli heard about his sons' behavior and from whom had he heard it?

INSIGHT

According to Deuteronomy 21:18–21, the Law of Moses instructed that if a son refused to obey when his father chastised him, or refused to even listen, the father was to bring his stubborn and rebellious son to the elders at the gate of the city, where they would stone him to death and thus remove evil from their midst.

1 SAMUEL 2:22–25

22 Now Eli was very old; and he heard all that his sons were doing to all Israel, and how they lay with the women who served at the doorway of the tent of meeting.

23 He said to them, "Why do you do such things, the evil things that I hear from all these people?

24 "No, my sons; for the report is not good which I hear the LORD's people circulating.

25 "If one man sins against another, God will mediate for him; but if a man sins against the LORD, who can intercede for him?" But they would

not listen to the voice of their father, for the LORD desired to put them to death.

• How did Eli respond to the reports of his sons' behavior? Was his response effective? Explain your answer.

• What should have been Eli's next step as Israel's spiritual leader and as the leader of his family?

• Describe the Lord's response to the sons' behavior. What does this reveal about the seriousness of the situation?

• Discuss what you learned about Eli's leadership as both a father and the high priest.

1 SAMUEL 2:27–35

27 Then a man of God came to Eli and said to him, "Thus says the LORD, 'Did I not indeed reveal Myself to the house of your father when they were in Egypt in bondage to Pharaoh's house?

OBSERVE

As a result of Eli's failure to deal with his sons' behavior, God sent a harsh message to him through an unknown messenger.

Leader: *Read aloud 1 Samuel 2:27–35. Have the group say aloud and mark the following:*

• *every reference to **Eli**, including pronouns, with an **E.***

- *every reference to **God**, including pronouns and synonyms, with a triangle:* △
- *the word **heart** like this:* ♡

DISCUSS

- What was Eli accused of doing in verse 29? Why was Eli held accountable for the actions of his sons? *He was dishonoring God by honoring his sons above God.*

  Because he was in chg.

- What leadership principle(s) can be learned from God's message to Eli? *We're to be an example leaders must be willing to do things that are uncomfortable*

  ★ We are asked to hold others accountable

  God holds us accountable.

28 'Did I not choose them from all the tribes of Israel to be My priests, to go up to My altar, to burn incense, to carry an ephod before Me; and did I not give to the house of your father all the fire offerings of the sons of Israel?

29 'Why do you kick at My sacrifice and at My offering which I have commanded in My dwelling, and honor your sons above Me, by making yourselves fat with the choicest of every offering of My people Israel?'

30 "Therefore the LORD God of Israel declares, 'I did indeed say that your house and the house of your father should walk

before Me forever'; but now the LORD declares, 'Far be it from Me—for those who honor Me I will honor, and those who despise Me will be lightly esteemed.

31 'Behold, the days are coming when I will break your strength and the strength of your father's house so that there will not be an old man in your house.

32 'You will see the distress of My dwelling, in spite of all the good that I do for Israel; and an old man will not be in your house forever.

33 'Yet I will not cut off every man of yours from My altar so that your eyes will fail from weeping and your soul

- The man of God gave a detailed picture of what would happen to the priesthood in Israel. Discuss the outcome prophesied in this passage for Eli's family.

Eli will not live a long life His sons would both die on the same day.

• Verse 35 begins with the word *but,* which signals a contrast. What was being contrasted in verse 34 and verse 35? Explain why this is significant.

> The old & new
> the wrong & the right.
> God will only
> that next faithful
> priest.

• What did you learn from marking *heart* in this passage, and what does this reveal about God's expectations of a leader?

> God has a heart
> of Compassion.
> We should strive
> to know his heart

grieve, and all the increase of your house will die in the prime of life.

34 'This will be the sign to you which will come concerning your two sons, Hophni and Phinehas: on the same day both of them will die.

35 'But I will raise up for Myself a faithful priest who will do according to what is in My heart and in My soul; and I will build him an enduring house, and he will walk before My anointed always.'"

OBSERVE

Even as Eli's sons were rebelling against God's ways, the high priest was given the responsibility of raising Samuel, a young child who had been given to God by his mother. God eventually called Samuel to

1 SAMUEL 3:11–14

11 The LORD said to Samuel, "Behold, I am about to do a thing in Israel at which both ears of everyone who hears it will tingle.

12 "In that day I will carry out against Eli all that I have spoken concerning his house, from beginning to end.

13 "For I have told him that I am about to judge his house forever for the iniquity which he knew, because his sons brought a curse on themselves and he did not rebuke them.

14 "Therefore I have sworn to the house of Eli that the iniquity of Eli's house shall not be atoned for by sacrifice or offering forever."

be a prophet to His people. Let's look briefly at the first of many personal conversations Samuel would have with God.

Leader: *Read aloud 1 Samuel 3:11–14. Have the group say aloud and mark…*

- *every reference to **the Lord,** including pronouns, with a triangle.* △
- *every reference to **Eli,** including pronouns, with an* **E.**

DISCUSS

- Discuss God's message to Samuel and what it confirmed.

  God will judge the house of Eli. The sin offering wouldn't last forever.

- Eli was not a contemptible priest like his sons, but he was the man in charge. Where did Eli fail in the leadership of not only his household but also the priesthood, according to this passage?

  He did not rebuke them. He didn't take the necessary actions.

OBSERVE

After God sent His message through Samuel, Eli and his sons lived for a short time. Hophni and Phinehas eventually were killed in a battle during which the Philistines seized the ark of the covenant, and Eli died upon hearing the news. His descendants continued to serve as priests for three generations; then the responsibility shifted to Zadok, a descendant of Aaron's son Eleazer, with whose line the priesthood remained throughout Israel's history. The time from Samuel's prophecy to fulfillment was approximately 130 years.

Leader: Read aloud 1 Samuel 3:15–20. Have the group…
- *draw a box around every reference to Samuel, including pronouns:* ▭
- *mark every reference to Israel, including pronouns, with a star:* ✡

DISCUSS

- What did you learn from marking *Samuel*?

He was a prophet
He told him
Samuel grew + God
was with him

1 SAMUEL 3:15–20

15 So Samuel lay down until morning. Then he opened the doors of the house of the LORD. But Samuel was afraid to tell the vision to Eli.

prophet
He will Abiaio la leea cei when he saw

16 Then Eli called Samuel and said, "Samuel, my son." And he said, "Here I am."

17 He said, "What is the word that He spoke to you? Please do not hide it from me. May God do so to you, and more also, if you hide anything from me of all the words that He spoke to you."

18 So Samuel told him everything and

hid nothing from him. And he said, "It is the LORD; let Him do what seems good to Him."

19 Thus Samuel grew and the LORD was with him and let none of his words fail.

20 All Israel from Dan even to Beersheba knew that Samuel was confirmed as a prophet of the LORD.

[handwritten annotation: North to the South]

JOSHUA 1:6–9

6 "Be strong and courageous, for you shall give this people possession of the land which I swore to their fathers to give them.

7 "Only be strong and very courageous; be careful to do according to all the

• Even though Samuel was a young boy and afraid to tell his mentor about his vision, how did he respond when Eli spoke to him? What does this tell you about his character and potential for leadership?

[handwritten: Samuel was respectful + truthful]

• Where did Eli recognize the word spoken to Samuel had come from?

[handwritten: It came from God himself]

• What verified the fact that Samuel was God's spokesman? Who recognized he was a prophet of the Lord?

[handwritten: all of Israel]

OBSERVE

We've seen how courage, or the lack of courage, affected the leadership of Eli and Samuel. As we bring this week to a close, let's look at a cross-reference where God talks about the importance of courage in the life of a leader. This passage details God's instructions to Joshua as he takes on the mantle of Israel's leader following the death of Moses.

Leader: Read aloud Joshua 1:6–9. Have the group do the following:

- *Draw a squiggly line under each occurrence of the phrase* **be strong and courageous:** ~~~~
- *Circle each occurrence of the pronouns* **you** *and* **your,** *which refer to Joshua.*
- *Mark every reference to* **success** *with an exclamation point:* **!.**

DISCUSS

- What did you learn by marking the phrase *be strong and courageous*? Who commanded it?

  God Commanded Joshua to be Strong & Courageous when God

- According to this passage, how would Joshua find success as a leader?

  Know the law & commandments Know the law, meditate continue to obey the law

- What evidence can you cite to support a connection between success and courage? Where would a leader today find courage? Discuss your answers.

  Know the Character of God & who he is, we begin to understand that he is loving Kind Gracious

law which Moses My servant commanded you; do not turn from it to the right or to the left, so that you may have success wherever you go.

8 "This book of the law shall not depart from your mouth, but you shall meditate on it day and night, so that you may be careful to do according to all that is written in it; for then you will make your way prosperous, and then you will have success.

9 "Have I not commanded you? Be strong and courageous! Do not tremble or be dismayed, for the LORD your God is with you wherever you go."

We Can handle anything.

WRAP IT UP

In examining these scenes from the lives of Eli and Samuel, we see that an effective leader must not only be willing to do what's right but also challenge others to do the same. This requires courage.

Eli exhibited a shameful lack of courage and strength when it came to his sons. He knew they had placed their own selfish desires ahead of their ministry to the people of God, yet he failed to discipline them effectively. He allowed their sinful actions to threaten the spiritual health of the people.

Samuel, by contrast, exhibited great courage as he delivered a hard message to Eli. He chose to obey the Word of God even at the risk of offending his mentor, with whom he clearly had a close relationship. Samuel not only had the courage to confront his mentor, he had the courage to confront the entire nation!

So we see that courage is an essential quality of effective leadership. Courage is not the lack of fear; it is the willingness to do what is right even in the face of fear. Such courage gives us the strength to confront those closest to us with the truth of God's Word. And where do we gain this courage? Through an intimate walk with God, as we'll see in the following weeks.

For now, the question to ask yourself is this: are you willing to step up wherever God has placed you and lead with strength and courage?

Last week we learned from Eli and Samuel that effective leadership requires courage and strength. Let's look further at Samuel's life to see what we can discover about the source of his courage and how he dealt with challenges to his leadership. As you read, remember to consider these principles in light of your own sphere of influence: in what capacity has God called you to lead, and how can these truths help you fulfill that role?

OBSERVE

In Samuel's first recorded public ministry following the death of Eli, he challenged the people to prove their loyalty to the Lord by abandoning their foreign gods and trusting in God alone for their protection and deliverance.

Leader: Read aloud 1 Samuel 7:3–6. Have the group do the following:

- *Draw a box around every reference to **Samuel,** including pronouns:* ☐
- *Draw a heart like this ♡ over every occurrence of the word **heart.***
- *Mark every reference to **the house of Israel** or **the sons of Israel,** including pronouns, with a star, like this:* ✡

1 SAMUEL 7:3–6

3 Then Samuel spoke to all the house of Israel, saying, "If you return to the LORD with all your heart, remove the foreign gods and the Ashtaroth from among you and direct your hearts to the LORD and serve Him alone; and He will deliver you from the hand of the Philistines."

⁴ So the sons of Israel removed the Baals and the Ashtaroth and served the LORD alone.

⁵ Then Samuel said, "Gather all Israel to Mizpah and I will pray to the LORD for you."

⁶ They gathered to Mizpah, and drew water and poured it out before the LORD, and fasted on that day and said there, "We have sinned against the LORD." And Samuel judged the sons of Israel at Mizpah.

DISCUSS

• What four things did Samuel instruct Israel to do in verse 3?

• What did he say would happen if they obeyed?

• How did the people respond to Samuel's instructions?

• Briefly describe what happened when Samuel gathered the people of Israel at Mizpah.

• Discuss the leadership principles Samuel demonstrated in this passage and how you might put these principles to work in your role as a leader.

OBSERVE

Leader: Read aloud 1 Samuel 7:7–11. Have the group do the following:

- Mark with a star any reference to **Israel,** including synonyms and pronouns.
- Draw a box around every reference to **Samuel,** including pronouns.
- Draw a triangle △ over every reference to **the Lord,** including pronouns.

DISCUSS

- At the height of Israel's humiliation and consecration at Mizpah, the lords of the Philistines went up against Israel. How did the sons of Israel respond, and what did they ask Samuel to do?

INSIGHT

The phrase *cry to the Lord* is used here as a synonym for *pray.*

1 SAMUEL 7:7–11

7 Now when the Philistines heard that the sons of Israel had gathered to Mizpah, the lords of the Philistines went up against Israel. And when the sons of Israel heard it, they were afraid of the Philistines.

8 Then the sons of Israel said to Samuel, "Do not cease to cry to the LORD our God for us, that He may save us from the hand of the Philistines."

9 Samuel took a suckling lamb and offered it for a whole burnt offering to the LORD; and Samuel cried to the LORD for Israel and the LORD answered him.

10 Now Samuel was offering up the burnt offering, and the Philistines drew near to battle against Israel. But the LORD thundered with a great thunder on that day against the Philistines and confused them, so that they were routed before Israel.

11 The men of Israel went out of Mizpah and pursued the Philistines, and struck them down as far as below Beth-car.

INSIGHT

Leviticus 1–7 describes in detail the various kinds of sacrificial offerings required by the Law of Moses. The phrase *whole burnt offering* indicates a particular sacrifice that represents the total dedication of the person offering it to the Lord.

• What did Samuel do, and what do you learn about leadership from his example?

• In verse 10 we see the phrase *but the LORD*. Sometimes in Scripture this phrase serves as a signal that God is about do something amazing. What did God do on this occasion, and what happened as a result?

OBSERVE

When the Philistines learned of the assembly, they attacked Israel at Mizpah, but the Lord defeated them in a mighty demonstration of power. In commemoration of this great triumph Samuel erected a monument that he called *Ebenezer,* which literally means "the stone of God's help."

Leader: Read aloud 1 Samuel 7:12–14. Have the group say aloud and...

- *draw a box around every reference to* **Samuel.**
- *underline every reference to* **_the Philistines,_** *including pronouns.*

DISCUSS

- Who did Samuel credit with defeating the Philistines?

- Why did Samuel do what he did, and what was the symbolism behind it?

- What did you learn about the Philistines in this passage?

- What did you learn about Samuel's leadership from this passage? How would you describe the extent of his influence? Explain your answer.

1 SAMUEL 7:12–14

12 Then Samuel took a stone and set it between Mizpah and Shen, and named it Ebenezer, saying, "Thus far the LORD has helped us."

13 So the Philistines were subdued and they did not come anymore within the border of Israel. And the hand of the LORD was against the Philistines all the days of Samuel.

14 The cities which the Philistines had taken from Israel were restored to Israel, from Ekron even to Gath; and Israel delivered their territory from the hand of the Philistines. So there was peace between Israel and the Amorites.

1 SAMUEL 8:1–10

¹ And it came about when Samuel was old that he appointed his sons judges over Israel.

² Now the name of his firstborn was Joel, and the name of his second, Abijah; they were judging in Beersheba.

³ His sons, however, did not walk in his ways, but turned aside after dishonest gain and took bribes and perverted justice.

⁴ Then all the elders of Israel gathered together and came to Samuel at Ramah;

⁵ and they said to him, "Behold, you have grown old, and your sons do not walk in your ways. Now

OBSERVE

Leader: Read aloud 1 Samuel 8:1–10. Have the group do the following:

- *Draw a box around every reference to **Samuel**, including pronouns.*
- *Mark every reference to **Israel**, including synonyms and pronouns, with a star.*
- *Mark every reference to **the Lord**, including pronouns, with a triangle.*

DISCUSS

- What did you learn about Samuel and his sons from this passage?

- What request did Israel make? Discuss why the people were concerned and the reasoning behind their request.

• How did Samuel feel about their request? What action did he take?

• What was God's response to Samuel's concerns? What did the Lord tell Samuel to do?

appoint a king for us to judge us like all the nations."

6 But the thing was displeasing in the sight of Samuel when they said, "Give us a king to judge us." And Samuel prayed to the LORD.

7 The LORD said to Samuel, "Listen to the voice of the people in regard to all that they say to you, for they have not rejected you, but they have rejected Me from being king over them.

8 "Like all the deeds which they have done since the day that I brought them up from Egypt even to this day—in that they have forsaken Me and

served other gods—so they are doing to you also.

9 "Now then, listen to their voice; however, you shall solemnly warn them and tell them of the procedure of the king who will reign over them."

10 So Samuel spoke all the words of the LORD to the people who had asked of him a king.

• How did Samuel respond to God's instructions? What does this reveal about his character as a leader?

• In Samuel's relationship to the Lord, what leadership principles have we seen?

---

1 SAMUEL 8:19–22

19 Nevertheless, the people refused to listen to the voice of Samuel, and they said, "No, but there shall be a king over us,

OBSERVE

Leader: Read aloud 1 Samuel 8:19–22. Have the group...

- *mark every reference to **the people of Israel,** including synonyms and pronouns, with a star.*
- *draw a box around every reference to **Samuel,** including pronouns.*

DISCUSS

• What did you learn about the people of Israel in this passage?

INSIGHT

The desire of the people was for a king so "that we also may be like all the nations" (1 Samuel 8:20). Yet God had called the nation of Israel to be different from all other nations. (See Leviticus 20:26; Deuteronomy 7:6.) Israel's direct relationship with God set the nation apart from others. In calling for a king, the people of Israel rejected God's direct rule and denied their unique heritage.

• What reasons did the people give for wanting a king to rule over them? What does this show us about their faith?

• Upon hearing their demand, what did Samuel do? What contrast does this reveal between Samuel's faith and the people's faith?

20 that we also may be like all the nations, that our king may judge us and go out before us and fight our battles."

21 Now after Samuel had heard all the words of the people, he repeated them in the LORD's hearing.

22 The LORD said to Samuel, "Listen to their voice and appoint them a king." So Samuel said to the men of Israel, "Go every man to his city."

• Compare Samuel's response with how you tend to react under pressure from others. What principles can you find in this passage for dealing with the demands of those under your leadership?

1 SAMUEL 12:1–5

¹ Then Samuel said to all Israel, "Behold, I have listened to your voice in all that you said to me and I have appointed a king over you.

² "Now, here is the king walking before you, but I am old and gray, and behold my sons are with you. And I have walked before you from my youth even to this day.

OBSERVE

As we'll read in next week's lesson, God directed Samuel to appoint the first king of Israel. As Samuel handed over the reins of leadership, he gave a farewell speech in which he reminded the people of their history, their responsibilities, and his own example of living with integrity.

Leader: *Read aloud 1 Samuel 12:1–5. Have the group...*

- *draw a box around every reference to* ***Samuel,*** *including pronouns.*
- *mark each occurrence of the word* ***witness*** *with a* **W.**

DISCUSS

• What did you learn from marking references to Samuel in this passage? At what point in his life was he giving this speech?

• What did you learn about Samuel's character as a leader from this passage?

• Contrast this description of Samuel with how those under your authority or influence would describe you and your leadership skills. Explain your answer.

³ "Here I am; bear witness against me before the LORD and His anointed. Whose ox have I taken, or whose donkey have I taken, or whom have I defrauded? Whom have I oppressed, or from whose hand have I taken a bribe to blind my eyes with it? I will restore it to you."

⁴ They said, "You have not defrauded us or oppressed us or taken anything from any man's hand."

⁵ He said to them, "The LORD is witness against you, and His anointed is witness this day that you have found nothing in my hand." And they said, "He is witness."

1 SAMUEL 12:7–17

7 "So now, take your stand, that I may plead with you before the LORD concerning all the righteous acts of the LORD which He did for you and your fathers.

8 "When Jacob went into Egypt and your fathers cried out to the LORD, then the LORD sent Moses and Aaron who brought your fathers out of Egypt and settled them in this place.

9 "But they forgot the LORD their God, so He sold them into the hand of Sisera, captain of the army of Hazor, and into the hand of the Philistines and into the hand of the king of

OBSERVE

After briefly discussing his leadership of Israel, Samuel gave the people a history lesson.

Leader: Read aloud 1 Samuel 12:7–17. Have the group say aloud and…
- *mark each reference to **the Lord,** including pronouns, with a triangle.*
- *draw a star over every reference to **the people** and **your fathers,** including pronouns.*

DISCUSS

- List and discuss all the things God had done for His people as described in this passage.

• What was the cause of the defeats Israel had suffered, and what response did each defeat provoke?

• By asking for a king, who had the people of Israel ultimately rejected as their leader?

Moab, and they fought against them.

10 "They cried out to the LORD and said, 'We have sinned because we have forsaken the LORD and have served the Baals and the Ashtaroth; but now deliver us from the hands of our enemies, and we will serve You.'

11 "Then the LORD sent Jerubbaal and Bedan and Jephthah and Samuel, and delivered you from the hands of your enemies all around, so that you lived in security.

12 "When you saw that Nahash the king of the sons of Ammon came against you, you said to me, 'No, but a king shall reign over

us,' although the LORD your God was your king.

13 "Now therefore, here is the king whom you have chosen, whom you have asked for, and behold, the LORD has set a king over you.

14 "If you will fear the LORD and serve Him, and listen to His voice and not rebel against the command of the LORD, then both you and also the king who reigns over you will follow the LORD your God.

15 "If you will not listen to the voice of the LORD, but rebel against the command of the LORD, then the hand of the LORD will be

• Despite Israel's stubbornness, what promise did God make through Samuel in verses 14–15?

• Discuss Samuel's declaration in verses 16–17. What was he hoping to accomplish and why? Explain your answer.

against you, as it was against your fathers.

16 "Even now, take your stand and see this great thing which the LORD will do before your eyes.

17 "Is it not the wheat harvest today? I will call to the LORD, that He may send thunder and rain. Then you will know and see that your wickedness is great which you have done in the sight of the LORD by asking for yourselves a king."

OBSERVE

Leader: Read aloud 1 Samuel 12:18–25. Have the group…
   • *mark every reference to **the people**, including pronouns, with a star.*
   • *draw a box around every reference to **Samuel**, including pronouns.*

1 SAMUEL 12:18–25

18 So Samuel called to the LORD, and the LORD sent thunder and rain that day; and all the people greatly feared the LORD and Samuel.

19 Then all the people said to Samuel, "Pray for your servants to the LORD your God, so that we may not die, for we have added to all our sins this evil by asking for ourselves a king."

20 Samuel said to the people, "Do not fear. You have committed all this evil, yet do not turn aside from following the LORD, but serve the LORD with all your heart.

21 "You must not turn aside, for then you would go after futile things which can not profit or deliver, because they are futile.

DISCUSS

• When the people witnessed the display of thunder and rain, a phenomenon unheard of during the wheat harvest, how did they respond?

• What specifically did the people ask Samuel to do, and what was his response?

• What character qualities of God are manifested in these verses?

• What leadership qualities does Samuel model in this passage? Look particularly at verse 23.

22 "For the LORD will not abandon His people on account of His great name, because the LORD has been pleased to make you a people for Himself.

23 "Moreover, as for me, far be it from me that I should sin against the LORD by ceasing to pray for you; but I will instruct you in the good and right way.

24 "Only fear the LORD and serve Him in truth with all your heart; for consider what great things He has done for you.

25 "But if you still do wickedly, both you and your king will be swept away."

WRAP IT UP

What a wealth of leadership principles we find in the life of Samuel!

One hallmark of Samuel's leadership was an active prayer life, a key priority for any godly leader. Throughout the Bible passages in this lesson we observed Samuel frequently talking to God. He asked for direction, listened for a response, and obeyed the Lord's instructions. Samuel also interceded with God on behalf of the people.

We see, too, that Samuel lived his life and led his people with integrity, even when those under his leadership made unwise demands. Rather than either lashing out in anger or caving in to pressure, he took his concerns directly to God and chose to be guided by His answer. And as he relinquished his role as the leader of Israel, though wounded and disappointed, Samuel refused to sin by ceasing to pray for the people.

Yet another characteristic of Samuel's leadership—communicating a clear vision—is evident in his farewell address to the people of Israel. Samuel was not just rehearsing history; he was reminding them of their unique calling as the people of God. His words remind us that an effective leader demonstrates the ability to give people a vision of who they are and what they are called to be.

What about you? How might following Samuel's example strengthen your effectiveness in your various leadership roles—as a parent or grandparent, supervisor, ministry leader, teacher, or group coordinator? Are you praying regularly for those under your care? Are you seeking God's solution to your challenges, or are you trying to muddle through on your own? And what witness does your life bear of your commitment to living with integrity and faith?

Have you ever found yourself unexpectedly thrust into a position of leadership? Have you at times felt inadequate to tasks to which God has called you? What actions can you take, what traits can you cultivate, if you're eager for God's blessing on your leadership? And how can you make wise decisions, even under intense pressure?

These are some of the questions we'll consider this week as we examine the strengths and weaknesses of Israel's first king.

OBSERVE

As we saw in last week's lesson, the people of Israel wanted to be like the other nations even though God had called them to be separate. After warning them of the cost, God granted their request. Let's meet the man who became Israel's first king. As you read, keep in mind that the man of God mentioned in this passage was the prophet Samuel.

Leader: Read aloud 1 Samuel 9:1–10. Have the group say aloud and...
- *circle each reference to **Saul**, including pronouns.*
- *draw a box around each reference to **man of God**, including synonyms and pronouns.*

1 SAMUEL 9:1–10

¹ Now there was a man of Benjamin whose name was Kish the son of Abiel, the son of Zeror, the son of Becorath, the son of Aphiah, the son of a Benjamite, a mighty man of valor.

² He had a son whose name was Saul, a choice and handsome man, and there was not a more handsome person than he among the sons of Israel; from

his shoulders and up he was taller than any of the people.

3 Now the donkeys of Kish, Saul's father, were lost. So Kish said to his son Saul, "Take now with you one of the servants, and arise, go search for the donkeys."

4 He passed through the hill country of Ephraim and passed through the land of Shalishah, but they did not find them. Then they passed through the land of Shaalim, but they were not there. Then he passed through the land of the Benjamites, but they did not find them.

DISCUSS

• What physical characteristics of Saul did you observe in this passage?

• What else did you notice about him?

• To whom did Saul turn for help in his search for his father's donkeys?

• What led him to this course of action?

5 When they came to the land of Zuph, Saul said to his servant who was with him, "Come, and let us return, or else my father will cease to be concerned about the donkeys and will become anxious for us."

6 He said to him, "Behold now, there is a man of God in this city, and the man is held in honor; all that he says surely comes true. Now let us go there, perhaps he can tell us about our journey on which we have set out."

7 Then Saul said to his servant, "But behold, if we go, what shall we bring the man? For the bread is gone

from our sack and there is no present to bring to the man of God. What do we have?"

8 The servant answered Saul again and said, "Behold, I have in my hand a fourth of a shekel of silver; I will give it to the man of God and he will tell us our way."

9 (Formerly in Israel, when a man went to inquire of God, he used to say, "Come, and let us go to the seer"; for he who is called a prophet now was formerly called a seer.)

10 Then Saul said to his servant, "Well said; come, let us go." So they went to the city where the man of God was.

- From what we learned last week, how well known was Samuel?

- What does Saul's conversation with his servant indicate about his spiritual awareness?

OBSERVE

Leader: Read aloud 1 Samuel 9:15–21. Have the group do the following:

- *Circle every reference to **Saul**, including pronouns.*
- *Mark every reference to **the Lord**, including pronouns, with a triangle.*
- *Draw a box around every reference to **Samuel**, including synonyms and pronouns.*

DISCUSS

- Discuss the conversation between the Lord and Samuel. What did you learn from marking the references to *the Lord*?

- What did you learn about Samuel from this interchange?

1 SAMUEL 9:15–21

15 Now a day before Saul's coming, the LORD had revealed this to Samuel saying,

16 "About this time tomorrow I will send you a man from the land of Benjamin, and you shall anoint him to be prince over My people Israel; and he will deliver My people from the hand of the Philistines. For I have regarded My people, because their cry has come to Me."

17 When Samuel saw Saul, the LORD said to him, "Behold, the man of whom I spoke to you! This one shall rule over My people."

18 Then Saul approached Samuel in the gate and said, "Please tell me where the seer's house is."

19 Samuel answered Saul and said, "I am the seer. Go up before me to the high place, for you shall eat with me today; and in the morning I will let you go, and will tell you all that is on your mind.

20 "As for your donkeys which were lost three days ago, do not set your mind on them, for they have been found. And for whom is all that is desirable in Israel? Is it not for you and for all your father's household?"

• What did you learn about Samuel from his conversation with Saul?

• What did you learn about Saul in this passage?

• What does Saul's response in verse 21 reveal about his character?

21 Saul replied, "Am I not a Benjamite, of the smallest of the tribes of Israel, and my family the least of all the families of the tribe of Benjamin? Why then do you speak to me in this way?"

OBSERVE

Saul stayed at the high place as Samuel's honored guest; then they went together to Samuel's house in town, where the two men conversed on the rooftop. At the close of their visit, Samuel walked with Saul and his servant to the edge of town.

Leader: Read aloud 1 Samuel 9:27–10:1. Have the group say aloud and…
  • *draw a box around every reference to* **Samuel,** *including pronouns.*
  • *circle every reference to* **Saul,** *including pronouns.*

1 SAMUEL 9:27–10:1

27 As they were going down to the edge of the city, Samuel said to Saul, "Say to the servant that he might go ahead of us and pass on, but you remain standing now, that I may proclaim the word of God to you."

10:1 Then Samuel took the flask of oil, poured it on his head, kissed him and said, "Has not the LORD anointed you a ruler over His inheritance?"

DISCUSS

• What event is described in these verses?

• Was this a public event or a private inter-action?

1 SAMUEL 10:17–24, 27

17 Thereafter Samuel called the people together to the LORD at Mizpah;

18 and he said to the sons of Israel, "Thus says the LORD, the God of Israel, 'I brought Israel up from Egypt, and I delivered you from the hand of the Egyptians and from the power of all the kingdoms that were oppressing you.'

19 "But you have today rejected your God, who delivers you from all your calami-ties and your dis-tresses; yet you have said, 'No, but set a

OBSERVE

Leader: *Read aloud 1 Samuel 10:17–24, 27. Have the group do the following:*
  • *Draw a box around every reference to* **Samuel,** *including pronouns.*
  • *Mark every reference to* **God,** *including synonyms and pronouns, with a triangle.*
  • *Circle every reference to* **Saul,** *including synonyms and pronouns.*

DISCUSS

• Discuss all that you learned in this pas-sage about Samuel and his message to the sons of Israel.

• What actions did you observe Saul taking in this passage?

king over us!' Now therefore, present yourselves before the LORD by your tribes and by your clans."

20 Thus Samuel brought all the tribes of Israel near, and the tribe of Benjamin was taken by lot.

21 Then he brought the tribe of Benjamin near by its families, and the Matrite family was taken. And Saul the son of Kish was taken; but when they looked for him, he could not be found.

22 Therefore they inquired further of the LORD, "Has the man come here yet?" So the LORD said, "Behold, he is hiding himself by the baggage."

23 So they ran and took him from there, and when he stood among the people, he was taller than any of the people from his shoulders upward.

24 Samuel said to all the people, "Do you see him whom the LORD has chosen? Surely there is no one like him among all the people." So all the people shouted and said, "Long live the king!"

27 But certain worthless men said, "How can this one deliver us?" And they despised him and did not bring him any present. But he kept silent.

• What does this indicate about his character? About his relationship with God?

• From what you've read, what sort of leader did Saul have the potential to become?

• What behavior did you observe in Samuel through this passage that shows his courageous leadership?

OBSERVE

Sometime after Samuel revealed God's choice for the leader of His people, Saul led a successful assault against the Ammonites, who had besieged the Israelite town of Jabesh-Gilead. His victory silenced his critics, and Saul officially took on the title and responsibilities of Israel's first king.

Leader: *Read aloud 1 Samuel 13:1–7. Have the group…*
- *circle every reference to **Saul**, including pronouns.*
- *mark every reference to **Israel**, including synonyms and pronouns, with a star.*

DISCUSS

- What did you learn from marking the references to Saul?

1 SAMUEL 13:1–7

¹ Saul was thirty years old when he began to reign, and he reigned forty two years over Israel.

² Now Saul chose for himself 3,000 men of Israel, of which 2,000 were with Saul in Michmash and in the hill country of Bethel, while 1,000 were with Jonathan at Gibeah of Benjamin. But he sent away the rest of the people, each to his tent.

³ Jonathan smote the garrison of the Philistines that was in Geba, and the Philistines heard of it. Then Saul blew the trumpet throughout

the land, saying, "Let the Hebrews hear."

4 All Israel heard the news that Saul had smitten the garrison of the Philistines, and also that Israel had become odious to the Philistines. The people were then summoned to Saul at Gilgal.

5 Now the Philistines assembled to fight with Israel, 30,000 chariots and 6,000 horsemen, and people like the sand which is on the seashore in abundance; and they came up and camped in Michmash, east of Beth-aven.

6 When the men of Israel saw that they were in a strait (for the people were hard-pressed),

- Who actually defeated the Philistines in Geba?

- Who took credit for defeating them?

- How did the Israelites respond to the Philistines gathering in Michmash?

• What conclusions can you draw about Saul's leadership style from this passage?

OBSERVE

Periodically, as leaders we face certain turning points, where the course of action we choose in a difficult situation can significantly strengthen or weaken our effectiveness. Let's watch to see how Saul responded under challenging circumstances.

Leader: *Read aloud 1 Samuel 13:8–14. Have the group…*
- *circle every reference to **Saul,** including pronouns.*
- *draw a box around every reference to **Samuel,** including pronouns.*

then the people hid themselves in caves, in thickets, in cliffs, in cellars, and in pits.

7 Also some of the Hebrews crossed the Jordan into the land of Gad and Gilead. But as for Saul, he was still in Gilgal, and all the people followed him trembling.

1 SAMUEL 13:8–14

8 Now he [Saul] waited seven days, according to the appointed time set by Samuel, but Samuel did not come to Gilgal; and the people were scattering from him.

9 So Saul said, "Bring to me the burnt offering and the peace offerings." And he offered the burnt offering.

10 As soon as he finished offering the burnt offering, behold, Samuel came; and Saul went out to meet him and to greet him.

11 But Samuel said, "What have you done?" And Saul said, "Because I saw that the people were scattering from me, and that you did not come within the appointed days, and that the Philistines were assembling at Michmash,

12 therefore I said, 'Now the Philistines will come down against me at Gilgal, and I have not asked the favor of the LORD.' So I forced myself and offered the burnt offering."

DISCUSS

• What had Samuel instructed Saul to do?

• What did Saul do instead?

INSIGHT

According to Leviticus 1–7, all sacrifices were to be carried out by a descendant of Aaron, of the tribe of Levi. In other words, only a priest was allowed to present a burnt offering. As we have seen, Saul was a member of the tribe of Benjamin.

• What justification did Saul give for his actions?

• Look again at verses 11–12. What attitude or concern seems to be at the heart of Saul's decisions?

• Sin always brings consequences. What did Samuel say would be the consequence of Saul's disobedience?

• Describe a situation in which you felt pressured to move ahead of God. How did you respond, and what was the outcome?

• What pressures are you facing today that are comparable to Saul's situation?

• What did you learn about Saul's leadership style from this passage?

13 Samuel said to Saul, "You have acted foolishly; you have not kept the commandment of the LORD your God, which He commanded you, for now the LORD would have established your kingdom over Israel forever.

14 "But now your kingdom shall not endure. The LORD has sought out for Himself a man after His own heart, and the LORD has appointed him as ruler over His people, because you have not kept what the LORD commanded you."

WRAP IT UP

Saul seemed to be perfectly suited to his leadership role. He was tall, strong, and handsome, not to mention humble. His own father was described as "a mighty man of valor" (1 Samuel 9:1). God had appointed Saul as king, the people approved of him, and Samuel was praying for him. What could possibly go wrong?

Signs of trouble were present early on: Saul hadn't learned to trust fully in God, so he never completely surrendered to His ways. For example, he knew through Samuel exactly what God had called him to do, but rather than stepping forward in faith at the appropriate moment, he hid in the luggage pile. Then again at Gilgal, he panicked while waiting for Samuel. Concerned that the people would flee, he violated the Law and offered the sacrifice himself. Saul's decisions were based on fear, not faith.

What about you? As you examine your leadership and your approach to challenges and decision making, ask yourself the following questions:

- *Can I honestly say I am totally surrendered to God?*
- *Is my leadership characterized by fear or faith?*
- *Do I give in to pressure from those I lead?*
- *Do I seek to find my own solutions, or do I seek God's solutions?*

Spend some time prayerfully considering these questions. Let God shine His holy light into the corners of your heart, and then respond in obedience to what He reveals.

Are you a leader or just the person out front? And do you know what makes the difference between the two?

Being a leader is fundamentally different from simply being a representative. A representative's job is to carry out, or follow, the will of the people. A leader, by contrast, sets a course for others to follow.

In a Christian context, a leader directs people down the path of obedience to God. This requires two things: First, the leader must be listening for God's voice. Second, the leader must have the courage and will to lead the people with authority, not simply represent them.

Let's look at how well Saul measured up to this standard of effective leadership.

OBSERVE

Long before Saul became king, the Amalekites savagely attacked Israel, an event God promised to avenge at the proper time. (See Exodus 17:8–16; Deuteronomy 25:17–19.) That time came during Saul's reign.

Leader: Read aloud 1 Samuel 15:1–9. Have the group say aloud and…
  - *circle every reference to **Saul**, including pronouns.*
  - *mark each occurrence of the words **destroy** and **destroyed** with a jagged line, like this: /W/*

1 SAMUEL 15:1–9

¹ Then Samuel said to Saul, "The LORD sent me to anoint you as king over His people, over Israel; now therefore, listen to the words of the LORD.

² "Thus says the LORD of hosts, 'I will punish Amalek for what he did to Israel, how he set himself against him on the

way while he was com-
ing up from Egypt.

3 'Now go and strike
Amalek and utterly
destroy all that he has,
and do not spare him;
but put to death both
man and woman, child
and infant, ox and sheep,
camel and donkey.' "

4 Then Saul sum-
moned the people and
numbered them in
Telaim, 200,000 foot
soldiers and 10,000
men of Judah.

5 Saul came to the
city of Amalek and set
an ambush in the valley.

6 Saul said to the
Kenites, "Go, depart,
go down from among
the Amalekites, so that
I do not destroy you
with them; for you
showed kindness to all

DISCUSS

• What did God, through Samuel, instruct
Saul to do?

• Was Saul obedient to those instructions?
Explain your answer.

• Based on what you read in verse 9, describe the apparent motivation behind Saul's actions.

• Discuss what you learned from this passage in regard to Saul's leadership.

• How important is complete obedience?

the sons of Israel when they came up from Egypt." So the Kenites departed from among the Amalekites.

7 So Saul defeated the Amalekites, from Havilah as you go to Shur, which is east of Egypt.

8 He captured Agag the king of the Amalekites alive, and utterly destroyed all the people with the edge of the sword.

9 But Saul and the people spared Agag and the best of the sheep, the oxen, the fatlings, the lambs, and all that was good, and were not willing to destroy them utterly; but everything despised and worthless, that they utterly destroyed.

1 SAMUEL 15:10–15

10 Then the word of the LORD came to Samuel, saying,

11 "I regret that I have made Saul king, for he has turned back from following Me and has not carried out My commands." And Samuel was distressed and cried out to the LORD all night.

12 Samuel rose early in the morning to meet Saul; and it was told Samuel, saying, "Saul came to Carmel, and behold, he set up a monument for himself, then turned and proceeded on down to Gilgal."

13 Samuel came to Saul, and Saul said to him, "Blessed are you

OBSERVE

We've seen that Saul failed to carry out God's instructions completely. As a leader, he might be expected to bear the responsibility for the actions of his people as well as for his own choices. Let's observe what happened when Saul was confronted about his decision.

Leader: Read aloud 1 Samuel 15:10–15. Have the group do the following:

- *Mark every reference to **the Lord,** including pronouns, with a triangle.*
- *Draw a box around every reference to **Samuel,** including pronouns.*
- *Circle every reference to **Saul,** including pronouns.*

DISCUSS

- What did you learn about God's emotions and concerns regarding Saul's leadership in this passage?

- How did Samuel respond to the Lord's words?

- After the battle, where had Saul gone, and for what reason?

INSIGHT

Gilgal was an important military staging site that also held great religious significance for the people of Israel during this era. This was the scene of Saul's earlier disobedience when Samuel instructed him to wait seven days for the prophet to present burnt offerings and peace offerings to God. Gilgal was also the place Saul was confirmed as king (1 Samuel 11:14).

- As Samuel approached Saul, who spoke first, and what did he say?

- What do the speaker's words reveal about the character of this man? Explain your answer.

- When confronted with the truth, how did Saul respond, and where did he place the responsibility?

of the LORD! I have carried out the command of the LORD."

14 But Samuel said, "What then is this bleating of the sheep in my ears, and the lowing of the oxen which I hear?"

15 Saul said, "They have brought them from the Amalekites, for the people spared the best of the sheep and oxen, to sacrifice to the LORD your God; but the rest we have utterly destroyed."

• Describe a time when you justified partial obedience. What was the outcome?

1 SAMUEL 15:16–23

16 Then Samuel said to Saul, "Wait, and let me tell you what the LORD said to me last night." And he said to him, "Speak!"

17 Samuel said, "Is it not true, though you were little in your own eyes, you were made the head of the tribes of Israel? And the LORD anointed you king over Israel,

18 and the LORD sent you on a mission, and said, 'Go and utterly destroy the sinners, the Amalekites, and fight against them until they are exterminated.'

OBSERVE

Leader: Read aloud 1 Samuel 15:16–23. Have the group do the following:

- *Circle every reference to **Saul,** including pronouns.*
- *Draw a triangle over every reference to **the Lord,** including pronouns.*
- *Mark every occurrence of the words **obey** and **obeying** with a big **O.***

DISCUSS

• What did God expect of Saul as the leader of His people?

• According to verses 22 and 23, how did Samuel characterize Saul's leadership?

- How would you characterize Samuel's leadership in this story?

- How did Saul respond when confronted with his disobedience?

- What was the consequence of Saul's actions as the leader of Israel?

- What conclusions can you draw from this passage about God's expectations of anyone who bears a responsibility to lead others?

19 "Why then did you not obey the voice of the LORD, but rushed upon the spoil and did what was evil in the sight of the LORD?"

20 Then Saul said to Samuel, "I did obey the voice of the LORD, and went on the mission on which the LORD sent me, and have brought back Agag the king of Amalek, and have utterly destroyed the Amalekites.

21 "But the people took some of the spoil, sheep and oxen, the choicest of the things devoted to destruction, to sacrifice to the LORD your God at Gilgal."

22 Samuel said, "Has the LORD as much delight in burnt offerings and sacrifices as in obeying the voice of the LORD? Behold, to obey is better than sacrifice, and to heed than the fat of rams.

23 "For rebellion is as the sin of divination, and insubordination is as iniquity and idolatry. Because you have rejected the word of the LORD, He has also rejected you from being king."

• Read verse 22 once more. In today's culture, what might be compared to the "burnt offerings and sacrifices" of Saul's day?

• From what you've read, how important is complete obedience to God's instructions? What can we learn from this that will make us better leaders?

OBSERVE

Leader: Read aloud 1 Samuel 15:24–35. Have the group do the following:

- *Circle every reference to **Saul**, including pronouns.*
- *Draw a box around every reference to **Samuel**, including pronouns.*
- *Draw a triangle over every reference to **the Lord**, including synonyms and pronouns.*

DISCUSS

- At this point how did Saul respond to Samuel's pronouncement of God's judgment?

- Based on what you read in this passage, was Saul truly repentant for all he had done? Explain your answer.

1 SAMUEL 15:24–35

24 Then Saul said to Samuel, "I have sinned; I have indeed transgressed the command of the LORD and your words, because I feared the people and listened to their voice.

25 "Now therefore, please pardon my sin and return with me, that I may worship the LORD."

26 But Samuel said to Saul, "I will not return with you; for you have rejected the word of the LORD, and the LORD has rejected you from being king over Israel."

27 As Samuel turned to go, Saul seized the edge of his robe, and it tore.

28 So Samuel said to him, "The LORD has torn the kingdom of Israel from you today and has given it to your neighbor, who is better than you.

29 "Also the Glory of Israel will not lie or change His mind; for He is not a man that He should change His mind."

30 Then he said, "I have sinned; but please honor me now before the elders of my people and before Israel, and go back with me, that I may worship the LORD your God."

31 So Samuel went back following Saul, and Saul worshiped the LORD.

• Discuss what Samuel did in verses 32–34 and any possible explanations for his actions.

• Who else was affected by Saul's leadership failure, and how were they affected?

• What did you learn about God's character from this passage?

• Thinking back over everything you've learned in the past three weeks, compare Samuel's leadership style with Saul's.

• What have you learned from their examples that you could apply to your own life? to your role as a leader?

32 Then Samuel said, "Bring me Agag, the king of the Amalekites." And Agag came to him cheerfully. And Agag said, "Surely the bitterness of death is past."

33 But Samuel said, "As your sword has made women childless, so shall your mother be childless among women." And Samuel hewed Agag to pieces before the LORD at Gilgal.

34 Then Samuel went to Ramah, but Saul went up to his house at Gibeah of Saul.

35 Samuel did not see Saul again until the day of his death; for Samuel grieved over Saul. And the LORD regretted that He had made Saul king over Israel.

WRAP IT UP

At the beginning of this week's lesson we posed this question: Are you a leader or just the person out front? We trust your study of Saul's life has shed some light on the difference between the two.

It seems obvious from what we've read that Saul failed the test of true leadership. Instead of listening to God's clear instructions and leading His people in complete obedience, Saul chose the path of partial obedience, blaming the people for his decision. God and Samuel both held Saul—not the people—accountable for disobeying God's instructions to destroy the Amalekites and everything associated with them. Why? Because God called Saul to be a leader, not just the man out front.

What about you? Do you accept responsibility for your failures as a leader, or do you blame others? Are you committed to obeying all the commands of the Lord or just the ones that seem convenient? Your answers to these questions determine whether or not you're truly being the leader God has called you to be.

In the past two weeks we've observed Saul's failures as a leader, failures that led God to reject him as king of Israel. In 1 Samuel 13:14 we read Samuel's declaration that Saul's kingdom would not endure. Instead, "the LORD has sought out for Himself a man after His own heart." With this description in mind, let's look at some passages that reveal exactly what kind of leader God was looking for.

OBSERVE

The Lord commissioned Samuel to anoint Saul's successor to the throne of Israel, but God, not Samuel, would do the choosing.

Leader: Read aloud 1 Samuel 16:1–13. Have the group do the following:
- *Mark each reference to **the Lord,** including pronouns and synonyms, with a triangle, as before.*
- *Mark a slash through each occurrence of **not chosen** and **rejected,** like this:*

- *Draw a heart over each occurrence of the word **heart.***

DISCUSS

- What did the Lord instruct Samuel to do?

1 SAMUEL 16:1–13

1 Now the LORD said to Samuel, "How long will you grieve over Saul, since I have rejected him from being king over Israel? Fill your horn with oil and go; I will send you to Jesse the Bethlehemite, for I have selected a king for Myself among his sons."

2 But Samuel said, "How can I go? When Saul hears of it, he will kill me." And the LORD said, "Take a heifer with you and

say, 'I have come to sacrifice to the LORD.'

3 "You shall invite Jesse to the sacrifice, and I will show you what you shall do; and you shall anoint for Me the one whom I designate to you."

4 So Samuel did what the LORD said, and came to Bethlehem. And the elders of the city came trembling to meet him and said, "Do you come in peace?"

5 He said, "In peace; I have come to sacrifice to the LORD. Consecrate yourselves and come with me to the sacrifice." He also consecrated Jesse and his sons and invited them to the sacrifice.

• What was Samuel's concern? Did that concern keep him from obeying the Lord? Saul wanted kill him. No this did not stop him from Obeying God.

• What was Samuel watching for as he waited on God to choose the next king of Israel? Samuel had a focus on the outward appearence & God was looking @ his Heart.

• How did this compare with God's selection criteria?

- Based on verse 7, what can we assume about the seven sons who passed before Samuel?

  There may have had great stature but the Lord looks @ the heart.

- Who was chosen to be Israel's next king, and what can you conclude about him based on this account?

  David - had a heart for God.
  He was the youngest + he wasn't into true religious practice + God was looking

- What are some of the characteristics we tend to identify with a leader?

  Bible knowledge (NOT)
  Appearance
  Character
  Integrity
  Well Spoken
  Charasmatic
  Should have X #'s
  Of yrs. of experience

6 When they entered, he looked at Eliab and thought, "Surely the LORD's anointed is before Him."

7 But the LORD said to Samuel, "Do not look at his appearance or at the height of his stature, because I have rejected him; for God sees not as man sees, for man looks at the outward appearance, but the LORD looks at the heart."

8 Then Jesse called Abinadab and made him pass before Samuel. And he said, "The LORD has not chosen this one either."

9 Next Jesse made Shammah pass by. And he said, "The LORD has not chosen this one either."

10 Thus Jesse made seven of his sons pass before Samuel. But Samuel said to Jesse, "The LORD has not chosen these."

11 And Samuel said to Jesse, "Are these all the children?" And he said, "There remains yet the youngest, and behold, he is tending the sheep." Then Samuel said to Jesse, "Send and bring him; for we will not sit down until he comes here."

12 So he sent and brought him in. Now he was ruddy, with beautiful eyes and a handsome appearance. And the LORD said, "Arise, anoint him; for this is he."

• How might those expectations cause us to miss God's best or ignore our own calling to leadership?

We put limitations on ourselves God will create + develop the leadership qualities use our gifts to serve God + the Church

• Discuss how this insight should be applied not only to those in leadership already, but also to the process of looking for a new leader.

Pray so that we don't miss a new leader
Do you have a willing heart?! God wants us to grow.

• What about you? Upon God's examination, would you qualify to be a leader?

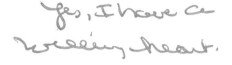

Yes, I have a willing heart.

OBSERVE

Sometime after David's anointing as Israel's future king—the precise timing is unclear—the Philistines came against Israel. Saul and Israel's army, including David's older brothers, met to battle the Philistines at the valley of Elah. A champion of the Philistines, Goliath, challenged Saul every day for forty days, saying, "I defy the ranks of Israel this day; give me a man that we may fight together" (1 Samuel 17:10). So terrifying was Goliath that he threw the army of Israel into a panic.

Leader: *Read aloud 1 Samuel 17:20–30.*
- *Have the group say aloud and mark every reference to **David**, including pronouns, with a **D**.*

13 Then Samuel took the horn of oil and anointed him in the midst of his brothers; and the Spirit of the LORD came mightily upon David from that day forward. And Samuel arose and went to Ramah.

1 SAMUEL 17:20–30

20 So David arose early in the morning and left the flock with a keeper and took the supplies and went as Jesse had commanded him. And he came to the circle of the camp while the army was going out in battle array shouting the war cry.

21 Israel and the Philistines drew up in battle array, army against army.

22 Then David left his baggage in the care of the baggage keeper, and ran to the battle line and entered in order to greet his brothers.

23 As he was talking with them, behold, the champion, the Philistine from Gath named Goliath, was coming up from the army of the Philistines, and he spoke these same words; and David heard them.

24 When all the men of Israel saw the man, they fled from him and were greatly afraid.

25 The men of Israel said, "Have you seen this man who is coming up? Surely he is coming up to defy

INSIGHT

The theory behind the kind of fight proposed by Goliath, as the Philistines' champion, was that the gods would grant victory to whichever man they chose. By allowing just two men to fight, each side minimized its loss of life. In this case, however, such a fight would have seemed a dangerous strategy for Israel: based on the description in 1 Samuel 17:4–7, scholars believe Goliath stood more than nine feet tall. He wore a bronze helmet and armor, which would have weighed approximately 150 pounds. The iron tip of his spear weighed approximately fifteen pounds. Considering only the physical evidence, the Israelite soldiers had great reason to fear Goliath.

DISCUSS

• Discuss all that you observed about David in this passage. *Brave / Bold*

Responsible
Eager
He loved & respected his brothers

• What was David's concern regarding Goliath and his challenge?

Who was Goliath you not part of God's chosen family. Who does Goliath think he is

• What accusation did Eliab, his oldest brother, make against David?

He said David was irresponsible insolent & wicked.

Israel. And it will be that the king will enrich the man who kills him with great riches and will give him his daughter and make his father's house free in Israel."

26 Then David spoke to the men who were standing by him, saying, "What will be done for the man who kills this Philistine and takes away the reproach from Israel? For who is this uncircumcised Philistine, that he should taunt the armies of the living God?"

27 The people answered him in accord with this word, saying, "Thus it will be done for the man who kills him."

28 Now Eliab his oldest brother heard when he spoke to the men; and Eliab's anger burned against David and he said, "Why have you come down? And with whom have you left those few sheep in the wilderness? I know your insolence and the wickedness of your heart; for you have come down in order to see the battle."

29 But David said, "What have I done now? Was it not just a question?"

30 Then he turned away from him to another and said the same thing; and the people answered the same thing as before.

• What might have been behind Eliab's anger? Jealousy.

OBSERVE

Saul was a warrior and, according to 1 Samuel 10:23, the tallest man in Israel. Not only did his size make him the logical choice to fight Goliath, but as king of Israel, Saul was responsible to lead the army to victory. Yet once again he lived by fear rather than faith.

Leader: *Read aloud 1 Samuel 17:31–40. Have the group do the following:*
- *Circle every reference to **Saul,** including pronouns.*
- *Mark every reference to **David,** including synonyms and pronouns, with a **D.***
- *Draw a heart over the word **heart.***

DISCUSS

- What did you learn about David from this passage?

1 SAMUEL 17:31–40

31 When the words which David spoke were heard, they told them to Saul, and he sent for him.

32 David said to Saul, "Let no man's heart fail on account of him; your servant will go and fight with this Philistine."

33 Then Saul said to David, "You are not able to go against this Philistine to fight with him; for you are but a youth while he has been a warrior from his youth."

34 But David said to Saul, "Your servant was tending his father's sheep. When a lion or a bear came and took a lamb from the flock,

35 I went out after him and attacked him, and rescued it from his mouth; and when he rose up against me, I seized him by his beard and struck him and killed him.

36 "Your servant has killed both the lion and the bear; and this uncircumcised Philistine will be like one of them, since he has taunted the armies of the living God."

37 And David said, "The LORD who delivered me from the paw of the lion and from the paw of the bear, He will deliver me from the hand of this Philistine." And Saul said to David, "Go, and may the LORD be with you."

• What did you learn about Saul?

• What training had David received as a warrior?

• In what ways might this training have prepared David to be a leader?

• In describing his battles to protect his father's flock from wild animals, to whom did David give the glory?

• Based on what you've read in this passage, describe David's relationship with and view of the Lord. Compare this with Saul's view of God.

38 Then Saul clothed David with his garments and put a bronze helmet on his head, and he clothed him with armor.

39 David girded his sword over his armor and tried to walk, for he had not tested them. So David said to Saul, "I cannot go with these, for I have not tested them." And David took them off.

40 He took his stick in his hand and chose for himself five smooth stones from the brook, and put them in the shepherd's bag which he had, even in his pouch, and his sling was in his hand; and he approached the Philistine.

1 Samuel 17:41–47

41 Then the Philistine came on and approached David, with the shield-bearer in front of him.

42 When the Philistine looked and saw David, he disdained him; for he was but a youth, and ruddy, with a handsome appearance.

43 The Philistine said to David, "Am I a dog, that you come to me with sticks?" And the Philistine cursed David by his gods.

44 The Philistine also said to David, "Come to me, and I will give your flesh to the birds of the sky and the beasts of the field."

OBSERVE

Leader: *Read aloud 1 Samuel 17:41–47. Have the group say aloud and...*

- *underline every reference to **the Philistine,** including pronouns.*
- *mark every reference to **David,** including pronouns, with a **D.***

Leader: *Read aloud the passage once more.*

- *Have the group say aloud and draw a triangle over every reference to **the Lord,** including synonyms and pronouns.*

DISCUSS

- What did you learn from marking references to *the Philistine?*

he had a big ego
He may have been
insecure (prideful
+ arrogant

- Contrast Goliath's words with David's. What message was each delivering to the other? Goliath was doing this battle & David knew God would fight the battle.

- According to verses 46 and 47, for what purpose would God deliver Goliath into David's hands? That all the earth would know there is a God. God doesn't have to fight c swords & spears.

- What does this interchange reveal about David? Where did his confidence lie, and how did this affect his behavior? Explain your answer. David's confidence was in God. He had courage in what God would do.

45 Then David said to the Philistine, "You come to me with a sword, a spear, and a javelin, but I come to you in the name of the LORD of hosts, the God of the armies of Israel, whom you have taunted.

46 "This day the LORD will deliver you up into my hands, and I will strike you down and remove your head from you. And I will give the dead bodies of the army of the Philistines this day to the birds of the sky and the wild beasts of the earth, that all the earth may know that there is a God in Israel,

47 and that all this assembly may know that the LORD does not deliver by sword or by spear; for the battle is the LORD's and He will give you into our hands."

• In your life and in your leadership, where does your confidence lie? What evidence can you give for your answer? In other words, how does the source of your confidence affect your personal behavior and your approach to leadership?

1 SAMUEL 17:48–53

48 Then it happened when the Philistine rose and came and drew near to meet David, that David ran quickly toward the battle line to meet the Philistine.

49 And David put his hand into his bag and took from it a stone and slung it, and struck the Philistine on his forehead. And the stone sank into his forehead, so that he fell on his face to the ground.

OBSERVE

Leader: *Read aloud 1 Samuel 17:48–53. Have the group say aloud and…*
   • *mark every reference to **David,** including pronouns, with a **D.***
   • *underline every reference to **the Philistine,** including synonyms and pronouns.*

DISCUSS

• What did you learn from marking references to *David*?

He did not hesitate

He did exactly what he said he was going to do

• How did he approach Goliath?

See Quest #1

c̄ confidence

He did his part

"He was in motion"

• What do David's actions reveal about his expectation of God?

He knew God would be with Him.

50 Thus David prevailed over the Philistine with a sling and a stone, and he struck the Philistine and killed him; but there was no sword in David's hand.

51 Then David ran and stood over the Philistine and took his sword and drew it out of its sheath and killed him, and cut off his head with it. When the Philistines saw that their champion was dead, they fled.

52 The men of Israel and Judah arose and shouted and pursued the Philistines as far as the valley, and to the gates of Ekron. And the slain Philistines lay along the way to Shaaraim, even to Gath and Ekron.

53 The sons of Israel returned from chasing the Philistines and plundered their camps.

1 SAMUEL 24:1–12, 15

1 Now when Saul returned from pursuing the Philistines, he was told, saying, "Behold, David is in the wilderness of Engedi."

2 Then Saul took three thousand chosen men from all Israel and went to seek David and his men in front of the Rocks of the Wild Goats.

3 He came to the sheepfolds on the way, where there was a cave; and Saul went in to relieve himself. Now David and his men were sitting in the inner recesses of the cave.

• What effect did David's action have on the Philistines? on the men of Israel?

*They fled – Philistine
The ran towards –
The Israelites*

OBSERVE

Soon after Goliath's defeat, Saul grew jealous of David, who quickly realized he must flee for his life. For the next several years Saul hunted obsessively for David, seeking to kill him.

Leader: Read aloud 1 Samuel 24:1–12, 15. Have the group…
- *circle every reference to **Saul,** including synonyms and pronouns.*
- *mark every reference to **David,** including pronouns, with a **D.***

DISCUSS

• How did Saul respond upon hearing that David was in the wilderness of Engedi?

*a while avve him
L took 3,000
men…*

• What did David's men conclude from the nearness and vulnerability of Saul in the cave? What was David's response?

• David's cutting off the edge of Saul's robe signified the transfer of power from the house of Saul to the house of David. With that in mind, why do you think David's conscience bothered him?

• David knew he was appointed to reign over Israel, so why wouldn't he take Saul's life?

4 The men of David said to him, "Behold, this is the day of which the LORD said to you, 'Behold; I am about to give your enemy into your hand, and you shall do to him as it seems good to you.'" Then David arose and cut off the edge of Saul's robe secretly.

5 It came about afterward that David's conscience bothered him because he had cut off the edge of Saul's robe.

6 So he said to his men, "Far be it from me because of the LORD that I should do this thing to my lord, the LORD's anointed, to stretch out my hand against him, since he is the LORD's anointed."

7 David persuaded his men with these words and did not allow them to rise up against Saul. And Saul arose, left the cave, and went on his way.

8 Now afterward David arose and went out of the cave and called after Saul, saying, "My lord the king!" And when Saul looked behind him, David bowed with his face to the ground and prostrated himself.

9 David said to Saul, "Why do you listen to the words of men, saying, 'Behold, David seeks to harm you'?

10 "Behold, this day your eyes have seen that the LORD had given you today into

• What does this passage indicate about David's understanding of God? about his own heart?

• How might having a similar perspective affect a leader's decisions today?

• Who had appointed Saul as king? By what authority would he be removed?

• What authorities has God placed over you?

• How do you respond when God places you under less-than-capable leaders? Have you ever tried to undermine someone's authority because you didn't respect that person or felt you would be a more effective leader?

Leader: Invite someone from the group to share a personal testimony, either positive or negative, and the result.

my hand in the cave, and some said to kill you, but my eye had pity on you; and I said, 'I will not stretch out my hand against my lord, for he is the LORD's anointed.'

11 "Now, my father, see! Indeed, see the edge of your robe in my hand! For in that I cut off the edge of your robe and did not kill you, know and perceive that there is no evil or rebellion in my hands, and I have not sinned against you, though you are lying in wait for my life to take it.

12 "May the LORD judge between you and me, and may the LORD avenge me on you; but my hand shall not be against you.

15 "The LORD therefore be judge and decide between you and me; and may He see and plead my cause and deliver me from your hand."

1 SAMUEL 24:16–22

16 When David had finished speaking these words to Saul, Saul said, "Is this your voice, my son David?" Then Saul lifted up his voice and wept.

17 He said to David, "You are more righteous than I; for you have dealt well with me, while I have dealt wickedly with you.

18 "You have declared today that you have done good to me, that the LORD delivered me into your hand and yet you did not kill me.

• Thinking back over all you've observed about David in this week's lesson, describe what it means to be a man after God's own heart and what that would look like in the life of a leader—a parent, a manager, a ministry head, a teacher—facing the challenges and temptations of today's culture.

OBSERVE

Leader: Read aloud 1 Samuel 24:16–22. Have the group…

- *circle every reference to **Saul,** including pronouns.*
- *mark every reference to **David,** including pronouns, with a **D.***

DISCUSS

• What effect did David's words have on Saul?

• What did Saul note about David's character? What difference did he recognize between the two of them?

• Saul acknowledged that David would be king and that Israel would be established in his hand. In light of this, what request did Saul make? How did David respond?

• What can we learn about leadership from David's response to Saul in the midst of what must have been a painful and difficult situation?

19 "For if a man finds his enemy, will he let him go away safely? May the LORD therefore reward you with good in return for what you have done to me this day.

20 "Now, behold, I know that you will surely be king, and that the kingdom of Israel will be established in your hand.

21 "So now swear to me by the LORD that you will not cut off my descendants after me and that you will not destroy my name from my father's household."

22 David swore to Saul. And Saul went to his home, but David and his men went up to the stronghold.

WRAP IT UP

What makes a leader? We've looked at many different characteristics of effective leadership in the past few weeks, but our study of David sums it all up in one powerful definition: a true leader is a man or woman after God's own heart.

The world's criteria for leadership might involve attending the right schools, living in the right neighborhood, coming from the right family, boasting the right socioeconomic status, having just the right look, or following the right systems. God, however, doesn't look on outward appearances when He places people in positions of leadership. Rather, He's concerned with issues of the heart.

David's life also demonstrates that developing the right heart attitude doesn't just happen; healthy hearts are shaped by God through times of trial and difficulty. David proved faithful to trust God in everything from ravaging bears and lions to murderous giants and kings. As challenges and crises confronted him, David acted on what he knew to be true about God, submitting to His authority and demonstrating courage and strength rooted in faith.

What about you? Is your life a witness to your intimate, personal knowledge of God? Does your leadership reflect a pursuit of God's heart and a confidence that He will work all things for your good and His glory?

Last week we observed the character qualities that made David both a great leader and "a man after [God's] own heart." However, David was by no means perfect, as we'll see in this week's lesson. His example reveals key insights for how to deal with our own inevitable failures as leaders—and emerge with a deeper knowledge of God.

OBSERVE

In week 5, we observed the character of young David, the shepherd boy and future king. Now let's fast-forward to a scene from midlife, after David had been on the throne of Israel for some time.

Leader: Read aloud 2 Samuel 11:1–5.
- *Have the group say aloud and mark every reference to **David,** including pronouns, with a **D.***

DISCUSS

- What time of year did this story take place? *Spring*

- What does verse 1 describe as the role of kings during this season? *Went out to battle*

2 SAMUEL 11:1–5

1 Then it happened in the spring, at the time when kings go out to battle, that David sent Joab and his servants with him and all Israel, and they destroyed the sons of Ammon and besieged Rabbah. But David stayed at Jerusalem.

2 Now when evening came David arose from his bed and walked around on the roof of the king's house, and from the roof he saw a woman bathing; and the

woman was very beautiful in appearance.

3 So David sent and inquired about the woman. And one said, "Is this not Bathsheba, the daughter of Eliam, the wife of Uriah the Hittite?"

4 David sent messengers and took her, and when she came to him, he lay with her; and when she had purified herself from her uncleanness, she returned to her house.

5 The woman conceived; and she sent and told David, and said, "I am pregnant."

• Where was King David?

He stayed home

• Briefly summarize the actions of David as described in this passage.

His eyes saw her + he lusted after her.

• What do these verses reveal about the priorities of David's heart?

His heart wasn't after God at this time. Was thinking after himself

• As you think back on the behavior and perspectives of David's early years, what contrasts do you observe?

OBSERVE

Leader: Read aloud 2 Samuel 11:6–13. Have the group…

- *mark every reference to **David**, including synonyms and pronouns, with a **D**.*
- *mark every reference to **Uriah**, including pronouns with a **U**.*

DISCUSS

- Briefly summarize David's actions in this passage and Uriah's corresponding responses.

He wanted him to go home & sleep c his wife

Uriah felt why should he have the comforts of going home to be with his wife. He was being honorable

2 SAMUEL 11:6–13

6 Then David sent to Joab, saying, "Send me Uriah the Hittite." So Joab sent Uriah to David.

7 When Uriah came to him, David asked concerning the welfare of Joab and the people and the state of the war.

8 Then David said to Uriah, "Go down to your house, and wash your feet." And Uriah went out of the king's house, and a present from the king was sent out after him.

9 But Uriah slept at the door of the king's house with all the servants of his lord, and did not go down to his house.

10 Now when they
told David, saying,
"Uriah did not go
down to his house,"
David said to Uriah,
"Have you not come
from a journey? Why
did you not go down
to your house?"

11 Uriah said to David,
"The ark and Israel and
Judah are staying in
temporary shelters, and
my lord Joab and the
servants of my lord are
camping in the open
field. Shall I then go to
my house to eat and to
drink and to lie with my
wife? By your life and
the life of your soul, I
will not do this thing."

12 Then David said
to Uriah, "Stay here
today also, and tomor-
row I will let you go."

• Discuss what you learned about David
and Uriah from this passage. How effectively did each man carry out his responsibilities? Explain your answer.

*He wasn't living up
to his responsibility.
Got him*

*Uriah was loyal ^honorable to the
King Servants & his
Soilders*

• Even though the word *heart* does not appear in this passage, compare the apparent differences between David's heart and
Uriah's heart as revealed in the events
detailed here.

*David   Verses Uriah
arrogant   was
deceitful   honor
                        & loyal
                        Serv*

OBSERVE

Up until this point David had hoped that Bathsheba's unborn child would be accepted as Uriah's, allowing his own adultery to remain hidden. When Uriah didn't cooperate with his scheme, David sank deeper into sin.

Leader: Read aloud 2 Samuel 11:14–18, 26–27. Have the group say aloud and mark…

- *every reference to **David,** including synonyms and pronouns, with a **D.***
- *every reference to **Uriah,** including pronouns, with a **U.***

DISCUSS

- Discuss the events of this passage.

  King David's betrayal
  + murder of Uriah
  perfect example of one little
  wrong turning into a laugh lie

- What was the ultimate goal behind David's instructions to Joab?

  Murder

So Uriah remained in Jerusalem that day and the next.

13 Now David called him, and he ate and drank before him, and he made him drunk; and in the evening he went out to lie on his bed with his lord's servants, but he did not go down to his house.

2 SAMUEL 11:14–18, 26–27

14 Now in the morning David wrote a letter to Joab and sent it by the hand of Uriah.

15 He had written in the letter, saying, "Place Uriah in the front line of the fiercest battle and withdraw from him, so that he may be struck down and die."

16 So it was as Joab kept watch on the city, that he put Uriah at the place where he knew there were valiant men.

17 The men of the city went out and fought against Joab, and some of the people among David's servants fell; and Uriah the Hittite also died.

18 Then Joab sent and reported to David all the events of the war.

26 Now when the wife of Uriah heard that Uriah her husband was dead, she mourned for her husband.

27 When the time of mourning was over, David sent and brought her to his

• What does David's plan of action reveal about the state of his heart? How would you characterize the motivations and emotions driving him?

Panic – what am I going to do.

His own sin has affe the lives of others.

• The Law called for the death of both parties involved in an adulterous relationship. Given the possible consequences for his adultery, what other options might David have pursued in this situation?

He could have Confessed this Sin before Uriah & God.

• From what you read in verse 27, what did the Lord think about this situation?

He felt it was evil.

OBSERVE

Leader: Read aloud 2 Samuel 12:1–14. Have the group say aloud and mark the following:

- *every reference to **Nathan,** including pronouns, with an **N.***
- *every reference to **David,** including pronouns, with a **D.***
- *every reference to **the Lord,** including pronouns, with a triangle.* △

DISCUSS

• Discuss what you learned from marking the references to *Nathan.*

God sent Nathan to shine a light on David's sin.
He was obedient

house and she became his wife; then she bore him a son. But the thing that David had done was evil in the sight of the LORD.

2 SAMUEL 12:1–14

1 Then the LORD sent Nathan to David. And he came to him and said, "There were two men in one city, the one rich and the other poor.

2 "The rich man had a great many flocks and herds.

3 "But the poor man had nothing except one little ewe lamb which he bought and nourished; and it grew up together with him and his children. It would eat of his bread

and drink of his cup and lie in his bosom, and was like a daughter to him.

4 "Now a traveler came to the rich man, and he was unwilling to take from his own flock or his own herd, to prepare for the wayfarer who had come to him; rather he took the poor man's ewe lamb and prepared it for the man who had come to him."

5 Then David's anger burned greatly against the man, and he said to Nathan, "As the LORD lives, surely the man who has done this deserves to die.

6 "He must make restitution for the lamb fourfold, because

• Who sent Nathan to David, and why?

God to reveal the secret

• What was David's initial response to Nathan's story?

He was outraged. He should of been killed.

• According to verses 7 and 8, by what means had David gained his position of power?

Through God God Picked him to be King Saved him from Sau He would have given them more.

• How does this relate to your own role as a leader? *God anointed us.*

• According to verse 9, what was the root issue in David's sin?

Despised the word of the Lord.

INSIGHT

Nathan said that David had "despised the word of the LORD" (verse 9), which means that he considered it lightly, failing to give proper weight to its authority. When we make decisions based on our own thinking and rationale rather than following God's standards and instructions, we despise the word of the Lord.

---

he did this thing and had no compassion."

7 Nathan then said to David, "You are the man! Thus says the LORD God of Israel, 'It is I who anointed you king over Israel and it is I who delivered you from the hand of Saul.

8 'I also gave you your master's house and your master's wives into your care, and I gave you the house of Israel and Judah; and if that had been too little, I would have added to you many more things like these!

9 'Why have you despised the word of the LORD by doing evil in His sight? You have struck down

Uriah the Hittite with the sword, have taken his wife to be your wife, and have killed him with the sword of the sons of Ammon.

10 'Now therefore, the sword shall never depart from your house, because you have despised Me and have taken the wife of Uriah the Hittite to be your wife.'

11 "Thus says the LORD, 'Behold, I will raise up evil against you from your own household; I will even take your wives before your eyes and give them to your companion, and he will lie with your wives in broad daylight.

• How exactly did God judge David's sin? What consequences did He set forth through Nathan?

will be in battle
His wives would ~~get~~ _be taken by other men out in Pub_

• How did David respond to Nathan's message of judgment?

He acknowledged his Sin.

• What does this response reveal about David's heart?

He repented.

• How did God respond when David took responsibility for his actions?

He spared his life + his son would surely die.

OBSERVE

In light of what we've just read, let's look back again at how Saul dealt with a similar failure.

Leader: Read aloud 1 Samuel 15:19–30. Have the group say aloud and...

12 'Indeed you did it secretly, but I will do this thing before all Israel, and under the sun.' "

13 Then David said to Nathan, "I have sinned against the LORD." And Nathan said to David, "The LORD also has taken away your sin; you shall not die.

14 "However, because by this deed you have given occasion to the enemies of the LORD to blaspheme, the child also that is born to you shall surely die."

1 SAMUEL 15:19–30

19 "Why then did you [Saul] not obey the voice of the LORD, but rushed upon the spoil and did what was evil in the sight of the LORD?"

20 Then Saul said to Samuel, "I did obey the voice of the LORD, and went on the mission on which the LORD sent me, and have brought back Agag the king of Amalek, and have utterly destroyed the Amalekites.

21 "But the people took some of the spoil, sheep and oxen, the choicest of the things devoted to destruction, to sacrifice to the LORD your God at Gilgal."

22 Samuel said, "Has the LORD as much delight in burnt offerings and sacrifices as in obeying the voice of the LORD? Behold, to obey is better than

• *circle each reference to **Saul**, including pronouns.*

• *draw a squiggly line like this ‿‿‿‿ under every reference to **God's instructions**, including **the voice of the Lord, the command of the Lord,** and **the word of the Lord.***

DISCUSS

• How did Saul respond when confronted with his sin? *He made excuses + blamed it on the people. He didn't take ownership.*

• Compare Saul's words in 1 Samuel 15:24 with David's confession of sin in 2 Samuel 12:13. How are the men's responses similar? How are they different?

sacrifice, and to heed than the fat of rams.

23 "For rebellion is as the sin of divination, and insubordination is as iniquity and idolatry. Because you have rejected the word of the LORD, He has also rejected you from being king."

24 Then Saul said to Samuel, "I have sinned; I have indeed transgressed the command of the LORD and your words, because I feared the people and listened to their voice.

25 "Now therefore, please pardon my sin and return with me, that I may worship the LORD."

26 But Samuel said to Saul, "I will not return with you; for you have rejected the word of the LORD, and the LORD has rejected you from being king over Israel."

27 As Samuel turned to go, Saul seized the edge of his robe, and it tore.

28 So Samuel said to him, "The LORD has torn the kingdom of Israel from you today and has given it to your neighbor, who is better than you.

29 "Also the Glory of Israel will not lie or change His mind; for He is not a man that He should change His mind."

• In the context of 1 Samuel 15, would you say that Saul's confession is genuine? Explain the evidence that supports your answer. VS. 30

• What does this tell you about Saul's relationship with God? In other words, what does it reveal about his heart?

He wasn't truly submitted to God.

OBSERVE

Let's look at Psalm 51, which David wrote after the prophet Nathan confronted him about his sin. As you read, remember the defining characteristic of God's chosen leader: "a man after His own heart" (1 Samuel 13:14).

Leader: Read aloud Psalm 51:1–4. Have the group say aloud and …
- *mark every reference to **God**, including pronouns, with a triangle.*
- *double underline every reference to **sin**, including synonyms like **transgressions** and **iniquity**.*

DISCUSS

• What did you learn from marking references to *sin* in this passage?

Sin is against God!

---

30 Then he said, "I have sinned; but please honor me now before the elders of my people and before Israel, and go back with me, that I may worship the LORD your God."

PSALM 51:1–4

1 Be gracious to me, O God, according to Your lovingkindness; according to the greatness of Your compassion blot out my transgressions.

2 Wash me thoroughly from my iniquity and cleanse me from my sin.

3 For I know my transgressions, and my sin is ever before me.

She understood the weight of her sin

4 Against You, You only, I have sinned and done what is evil in Your sight, so that You are justified when You speak and blameless when You judge.

• What was David doing in these verses? Describe the state of his heart and his attitude toward God. *Repenting & mournful*

• List some of the characteristics David attributed to God. *Justified, gra Blameless, compassion loving kindness Fai*

• What light do these characteristics shed on David's situation? on his perspective about his sin? *Anything God does he is justified & blamel*

PSALM 51:5–13

5 Behold, I was brought forth in iniquity, and in sin my mother conceived me.

6 Behold, You desire truth in the innermost being, and in the hidden part You will make me know wisdom.

7 Purify me with hyssop, and I shall be clean; wash me, and I shall be whiter than snow.

OBSERVE

Let's continue looking at David's prayer of repentance.

Leader: Read aloud Psalm 51:5–13. Have the group do the following:

- *Mark each pronoun referring to **David** with a **D**.*
- *Double underline each occurrence of **sin** and its synonyms.*
- *Draw a triangle over every reference to **God**, including pronouns.*

DISCUSS

- What did David believe God desired of him? *Truth in our innermost being*

- What did David ask of God? What does this tell you about his heart? *Purify him (wanted back in relationship c̄ God)*

- From what you have observed about David, how would you describe him? What are his strengths and weaknesses as a leader? *He humbled himself & cried out to God.*

- Do you have to be perfect to have a heart for God? Explain your answer. *NO*

- Neither of Israel's first two kings was perfect, but even with his flaws David "found favor in God's sight" (Acts 7:46) and was described by God as "a man after my heart" (Acts 13:22). What made the difference between David and Saul? Explain your answer. *humility & a true repentful heart*

8 Make me to hear joy and gladness, let the bones which You have broken rejoice.

9 Hide Your face from my sins and blot out all my iniquities.

10 Create in me a clean heart, O God, and renew a steadfast spirit within me.

11 Do not cast me away from Your presence and do not take Your Holy Spirit from me.

12 Restore to me the joy of Your salvation and sustain me with a willing spirit.

13 Then I will teach transgressors Your ways, and sinners will be converted to You.

his was his passion for God.

only focused on God.

WRAP IT UP

During a recent visit home from her secular college, our daughter told us that her literature teacher just could not understand why the Bible would call David "a man after [God's] own heart." He noted that David was, after all, a rapist and a murderer. When we asked how she answered the teacher's question, our daughter responded, "He repented."

Her answer reveals the key characteristic that separates Israel's first two kings—and that separates any great leader apart from the rest.

As we've seen, both Saul and David sinned, and both were confronted by prophets of God. One refused to accept responsibility for his actions; the other repented. Their responses made all the difference in how God viewed them. David remained a man after God's own heart not because he was perfect but because he repented.

Their examples confirm that all leaders make mistakes. But great leaders admit their failures, learn from them, and try not to repeat them.

We find another, more subtle principle of leadership in the first verse of this lesson: "Then it happened in the spring, at the time when kings go out to battle, that David sent Joab and his servants with him and all Israel, and they destroyed the sons of Ammon and besieged Rabbah. But David stayed at Jerusalem" (2 Samuel 11:1).

Instead of leading his troops in combat, the king sent someone else to do his job. David set himself up for failure by not being where he should have been. Too many leaders let their guard down when things seem to be going well. This is when the enemy attacks.

As we conclude our study of leadership, let's remember that as followers of Christ, we are to be diligent in leading wherever God has placed us. We are called to be light in a dark world, leading others to the Way, the Truth, and the Life—to Jesus Christ. We are called to be leaders in our homes, our workplaces, and our communities. Many of us are also called to be leaders in our churches or other avenues of ministry.

Will you lead with courage and strength, seeking to please God no matter what others pressure you to do? Will you maintain an active, vibrant prayer life, listening carefully for God's voice? Will you walk in faith and obedience, humbly taking responsibility for your decisions and repenting when you make mistakes? Will you motivate those under your leadership to capture a vision for following God?

Will you be a leader after God's own heart?

40 MINUTE BIBLE STUDIES

No-Homeworl

That Help Yc

A 6-WEEK, NO-HOMEWORK BIBLE STUDY
MORE THAN 700,000 SOLD IN THE SERIES

Being a Disciple: Counting the Real Cost

Kay Arthur, Tom & Jane Hart

PRECEPT MINISTRIES INTERNATIONAL

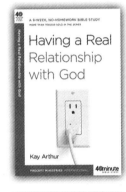

A 6-WEEK, NO-HOMEWORK BIBLE STUDY
MORE THAN 700,000 SOLD IN THE SERIES

Having a Real Relationship with God

Kay Arthur

PRECEPT MINISTRIES INTERNATIONAL

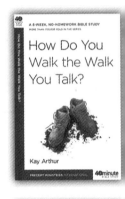

A 6-WEEK, NO-HOMEWORK BIBLE STUDY
MORE THAN 700,000 SOLD IN THE SERIES

How Do You Walk the Walk You Talk?

Kay Arthur

PRECEPT MINISTRIES INTERNATIONAL

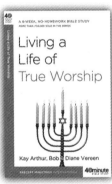

A 6-WEEK, NO-HOMEWORK BIBLE STUDY
MORE THAN 700,000 SOLD IN THE SERIES

Living a Life of True Worship

Kay Arthur, Bob & Diane Vereen

PRECEPT MINISTRIES INTERNATIONAL

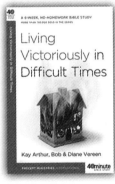

A 6-WEEK, NO-HOMEWORK BIBLE STUDY
MORE THAN 700,000 SOLD IN THE SERIES

Living Victoriously in Difficult Times

Kay Arthur, Bob & Diane Vereen

PRECEPT MINISTRIES INTERNATIONAL

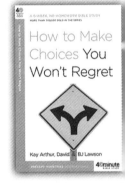

A 6-WEEK, NO-HOMEWORK BIBLE STUDY
MORE THAN 700,000 SOLD IN THE SERIES

How to Make Choices You Won't Regret

Kay Arthur, David & BJ Lawson

PRECEPT MINISTRIES INTERNATIONAL

A 6-WEEK, NO-HOMEWORK BIBLE STUDY
MORE THAN 700,000 SOLD IN THE SERIES

Money and Possessions: The Quest for Contentment

Kay Arthur & David Arthur

PRECEPT MINISTRIES INTERNATIONAL

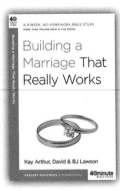

A 6-WEEK, NO-HOMEWORK BIBLE STUDY
MORE THAN 700,000 SOLD IN THE SERIES

Building a Marriage That Really Works

Kay Arthur, David & BJ Lawson

PRECEPT MINISTRIES INTERNATIONAL

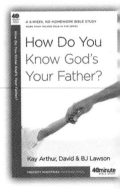

A 6-WEEK, NO-HOMEWORK BIBLE STUDY
MORE THAN 700,000 SOLD IN THE SERIES

How Do You Know God's Your Father?

Kay Arthur, David & BJ Lawson

PRECEPT MINISTRIES INTERNATIONAL

Bible Studies
Discover Truth For Yourself

Discovering
What the
Future Holds

Kay Arthur & Georg Huber

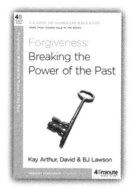

Forgiveness:
Breaking the
Power of the Past

Kay Arthur, David & BJ Lawson

Living Like
You Belong
to God

Kay Arthur, David & BJ Lawson

The Essentials
of Effective
Prayer

Kay Arthur, David & BJ Lawson

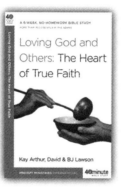

Loving God and
Others: The Heart
of True Faith

Kay Arthur, David & BJ Lawson

Understanding
Spiritual Gifts

Kay Arthur, David and BJ Lawson

Also Available:
A Man's Strategy for Conquering Temptation
Rising to the Call of Leadership
Key Principles of Biblical Fasting
What Does the Bible Say About Sex?
Turning Your Heart Toward God
Fatal Distractions: Conquering Destructive Temptations
Spiritual Warfare: Overcoming the Enemy
The Power of Knowing God
Breaking Free from Fear

Another powerful study series
from beloved Bible teacher

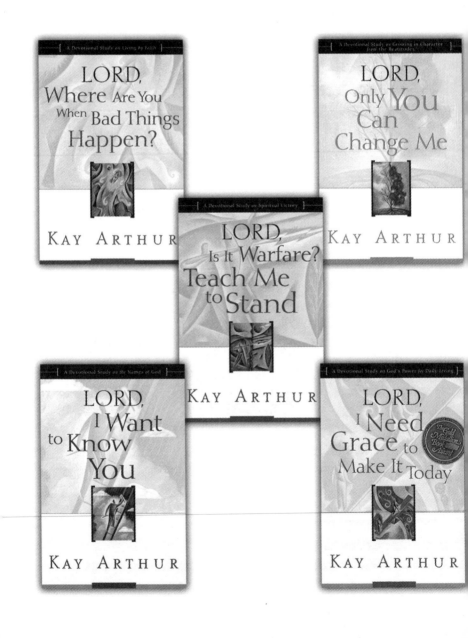

KAY ARTHUR

The Lord series provides insightful, warm-hearted Bible studies designed to meet you where you are —and help you discover God's answers to your deepest needs.

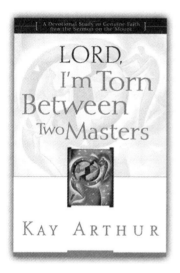

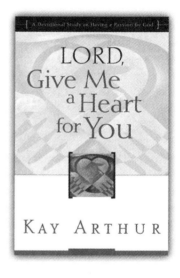

ALSO AVAILABLE:
One-year devotionals to draw you closer to the heart of God.

ABOUT KAY ARTHUR AND PRECEPT MINISTRIES INTERNATIONAL

KAY ARTHUR is known around the world as an international Bible teacher, author, conference speaker, and host of the national radio and television programs *Precepts for Life,* which reaches a worldwide viewing audience of over 94 million. A four-time Gold Medallion Award–winning author, Kay has authored more than 100 books and Bible studies.

Kay and her husband, Jack, founded Precept Ministries International in 1970 in Chattanooga, Tennessee, with a vision to establish people in God's Word. Today, the ministry has a worldwide outreach. In addition to inductive study training workshops and thousands of small-group studies across America, PMI reaches nearly 150 countries with inductive Bible studies translated into nearly 70 languages, teaching people to discover Truth for themselves.

Contact Precept Ministries International for more information about inductive Bible studies in your area.

Precept Ministries International
P.O. Box 182218
Chattanooga, TN 37422-7218
800-763-8280
www.precept.org

ABOUT DAVID AND BJ LAWSON

DAVID AND BJ LAWSON have been involved with Precept Ministries International since 1980. After nine years in the pastorate, they joined PMI full-time as directors of the student ministries and staff teachers and trainers. A featured speaker at PMI conferences and in Precept Upon Precept videos, David writes for the Precept Upon Precept series, the New Inductive Study Series, and the 40-Minute Bible Studies series. BJ has written numerous 40-Minute Bible Studies and serves as the chief editor and developer of the series. In addition she is a featured speaker at PMI women's conferences.